MW01442960

The Shattered Cedar:
A Brief of Lebanon's Wars
1975 - 2006

© 2023 Spoken Dialects LLC. All rights reserved.

No part of this publication may be reproduced, distributed, or transmitted in any form or by any means, including photocopying, recording, or other electronic or mechanical methods, without the prior written permission of the publisher, except in the case of brief quotations embodied in critical reviews and certain other noncommercial uses permitted by copyright law.

This copyright notice applies to all copies of the work and any portions thereof.

To the resilient souls who endured the hardships of Lebanon's wars, and to the memory of those who are still missing...

Table of Contents

The Birth of Modern Lebanon 9

The Conflict Begins 15

The Final Countdown 18

Country in Turmoil 23

Syria Enters the Lebanese Civil War 25

The Fire Spreads 28

The Rising New Parties 35

Israel Invades 39

Arab Capital is Down 42

The Bloodshed 47

The Retreat 50

Rivalries 56

Syria is Back 62

The Solution Must Arrive 67

Ending the War 70

The Aftermath: 1990-2000 Southern Conflict ... 75

The Withdrawal: 2000 83

The 2006 33 Day War 86

The Birth of Modern Lebanon

Lebanon emerged as the world knows it today, following the reorganization of the Middle East after World War I, with the region previously under Ottoman rule being apportioned among the victorious allies.

Proclamation of Greater Lebanon in Beirut, c.1920.

In 1920, the allies placed Lebanon under French oversight, enlarging its territory by taking parts from Syria. The country became a melting pot of diverse religious communities, including Christian Maronites, Orthodox and Armenians, as well as Muslim Sunnites, Shiites, and Druzes, among others. Due to the strong desire for autonomy among the Lebanese people, supported by Winston

Churchill's government in London, Paris was compelled to grant Lebanon its independence in 1943.

Bechara El Khoury and his government, led by Ryad El Soleh, devised an arrangement that acknowledged the country's religious sensitivities, allocating the presidency to Christian Maronites, the head of parliament to Muslim Shiites, and the prime ministerial role to Sunnites.

This understanding, known as the "National Pact," laid the foundation for modern-day Lebanon, uniting the various religious denominations in the country. It was established as an oral agreement, shaping a confessional compromise that determined Lebanon's Arabic identity and its independent foreign policy. This compromise was marked by Muslims relinquishing their call for permanent unity with Syria, while Christians renounced the desire for foreign protection.

The National Pact was widely viewed as crucial for Lebanon's survival, although many argued that it required further reinforcement to prevent future challenges. In 1952, President El Khoury was overthrown following widespread protests over allegations of corruption and nepotism. Kamil Chamoun assumed the presidency, coinciding with the rise of a young officer who would become a symbolic leader for millions of Arabs for the next two decades.
Amid the global divide of the Cold War between the USA and the USSR, Lebanon found itself open to regional and international influences, with competing movements vying for dominance in the Arab world. While the West sought to contain communist expansion, some advocated for Arab unity, leading to geopolitical tensions and alliances.

Tensions escalated in 1956 when Jamal Abd El Nasser nationalized the Suez Canal, prompting military intervention by Britain, France, and Israel. President Chamoun, aiming to mediate the crisis, called for an emergency meeting of Arab states in Beirut, as global powers jockeyed for influence in the region.

Abd El Nasser's increasing popularity posed a challenge to established systems in the Arab world, while US President Dwight Eisenhower presented a series of measures to enable military intervention against Soviet influence, further complicating the regional dynamics.

In Lebanon, the opposition clashed with Eisenhower's principles, leading to a joint Lebanese-American communique. This declaration signified Lebanon's approval of President Chamoun's support for Eisenhower's project, particularly in light of concerns raised by the Egyptian President's statement. The opposition's dissent extended beyond foreign policy to internal demands, including a call for an increase in Parliament seats. Despite this opposition, the election law submitted by the government was ultimately ratified, resulting in tense parliamentary elections that culminated in a victory for President Chamoun.

Following this, fresh controversy emerged as the opposition accused President Chamoun of seeking to amend the constitution to prolong his tenure. This discord coincided with escalating regional tensions, with Syria accusing Lebanon of conspiring against it through Baghdad's Alliance.

These regional dynamics ultimately led to the formation of the United Arab Republic by Egypt and Syria, a development that elicited divergent reactions within Lebanon. The relationship between the government and the opposition deteriorated, with opposition newspapers becoming platforms for fierce criticism of President Chamoun. Hostility erupted into tragedy when a prominent opposition journalist, Nasib El Matni, was assassinated, amplifying an already volatile situation. As the country teetered on the brink of war, the Lebanese Army grappled with the delicate balance of thwarting attempts to overthrow President Chamoun without exacerbating divisions within the country.

Meanwhile, the international community became embroiled in Lebanon's turmoil, with the United Nations (UN) scrutinizing allegations of external meddling. Amid these challenges, rumors of potential American intervention swirled, further complicating an already tumultuous situation.

As the crisis deepened, international events, including a coup d'état in Iraq, sent shockwaves through the Middle East, prompting President Dwight Eisenhower to announce the deployment of Marines to Lebanon. Upon the silent arrival of the marines on the Lebanese shores, the Americans recognized the crucial role played by President Fouad Chehab in upholding security and order during their deployment. With adept diplomacy, Chehab navigated the complexities of Lebanese politics, maintaining friendly ties with Washington and Cairo. Meanwhile, American delegate

Robert Murphy tirelessly shuttled between Beirut and Cairo in search of a successor to President Chamoun.

Following a period of upheaval, General Fouad Chehab was elected as Lebanon's new president on July 31st, succeeding Kamil Chamoun. The country gradually found stability under Chehab's leadership, marked by his inclusive "no winners nor losers" approach. However, unrest flared up as the Phalanges Party and Chamoun loyalists launched a counterrevolution, catching the new president off guard. The crisis was defused with the formation of a balanced fourfold government led by Karameh, putting an end to the counterrevolution. President Chehab's most notable moment in office came during a meeting with President Abd El Nasser at the Lebanese-Syrian border, where he pledged to prevent anti-United Arab Republic activities in Lebanon, while receiving Nasser's unwavering support for Lebanese unity.

Internally, calls for a more representative parliament led to a return of opposition leaders in the 1960 elections. President Chehab surprised many by announcing his resignation, asserting that he had guided Lebanon through its crisis and his presence was no longer essential. Amid accusations of political maneuvering, he eventually retracted his resignation, laying the groundwork for a new era in Lebanon.

Under his leadership, vital institutions such as the Lebanese Bank, Civil Service Council, and National Fund for Social Security were established. President Chehab also focused on extending essential services like electricity and healthcare to previously overlooked areas, elevating his stature and political influence to unprecedented levels. This period came to be known as the Chehabian Course, shaping Lebanon's future.

The Conflict Begins

On June 5th, 1967, the Arabs suffered a devastating defeat, marking a significant blow in their modern history. The loss of what remained of Palestine fueled the Palestinians' determination to take up arms and fight for their nation's freedom. Three years before the June war, the Arabs had established the Palestine Liberation Organization, but the shattering defeat pushed the situation beyond their control, leading to the rise of the legend of the Palestinian Fedayeen as the once towering figure of Abd El Nasser began to falter.

The organization initially settled in Jordan but later shifted operations to Lebanon during a period of significant growth for the country. Despite President Chehab's efforts to restore stability, the growing authority of the Second Division and the Lebanese Army Secret Services resulted in heightened criticism of what was perceived as a police rule, particularly within the Palestinian camps.

Tensions continued to escalate, and on December 28th, 1968, an Israeli strike on Beirut's International Airport further strained relations. The international community became involved, with a meeting held by the International Security Council in New York to address Lebanon's complaint, while a survey by El-Nahar Newspaper revealed continued support for the Fedayeen operations among most Lebanese people.

Amid the backdrop of global political shifts and internal turmoil in Lebanon, efforts were made to prevent further battles between the Army and the Fedayeen. However, violent clashes erupted in 1969, spreading from Nahr el-Bared camp in the North to other regions, prompting the resignation of Prime Minister Rachid Karameh and intervention by Syria's Sallah Jadid.

Efforts to resolve the crisis led to a Lebanese delegation meeting with the head of the Palestine Liberation Organization, Yasser Arafat, in Cairo, resulting in a contentious treaty. Despite initial approval from all Lebanese sides, doubts arose among the right-wing, and the treaty ultimately failed due to an essential flaw.

A new Lebanese government was formed, with efforts made to maintain internal stability, culminating in four crucial events in 1970 that would shape the region's trajectory for the next two decades. These events included the "Black September" in Jordan, following which President Abd El Nasser's efforts to promote Palestinian-Jordanian reconciliation in Cairo were tragically cut short by his untimely passing.In the complex political landscape of the

1970s, significant events unfolded in Syria and Lebanon that would shape the region for years to come. A coup d'état in Syria led by Defense Minister Hafez El Assad, disguised as a "Reform Movement," ousted influential figures like Salah Jadid and Presidents Nour El Dinh Atassy. Meanwhile, in Lebanon, the election of President Franjieh, with close ties to El Assad, sparked tensions and power struggles, with decisions and actions triggering a series of regrettable consequences.

Lebanon found itself caught in the crossfire of international conflicts, as the Palestinian presence grew stronger and Israel retaliated with force. Tragically, violent incidents claimed the lives of prominent figures, fuelling further strife and polarization.

The turmoil reached a boiling point, leading to internal chaos and conflict, resulting in resignations and a dangerous escalation of violence. Efforts to broker agreements and reconciliation faltered amid deep divisions, further fueling animosity and suspicion.

As the country teetered on the brink of crisis, Lebanon found itself mired in internal and external struggles, and the sense of impending catastrophe loomed ominously over the nation, despite outward displays of celebration and independence.

The Final Countdown

The countdown began in Lebanon for the outbreak of war, as both sides prepared for the impending battle with the armed Palestinians. The Lebanese Right had been training their forces since 1970, but the crisis was not solely due to the Palestinian issue. The left strongly advocated for political reform in the country, seeking to abolish political sectarianism and ensure equal representation in Parliament, with 6 seats allotted for Christians and 5 for Muslims. However, Christian Maronite leaders opposed these reform demands, while Muslims, in general, and the Lebanese left in particular supported them, viewing Palestinians as natural allies.

In 1974, clashes erupted between the Fedayeen and the Phalanges Party in Dekwaneh, near the Tal El – Za'atar Camp, leading to harassment of some Lebanese individuals, including Bachir, son of Pierre El Jemayel, founder of the Phalanges Party.

The following year, a significant turning point occurred in Lebanon when fishermen in the city of Sayda protested against the government's exclusive fishing rights granted to a company. Tensions escalated, resulting in firing at the demonstrators, and the leader of the Popular Naserian organization, Ma'rouf Sa'd, was fatally shot. This incident led to further demonstrations and unrest in Sayda and Beirut.

Ain el Remmaneh bus that sparked the civil war

In the early hours of April 13, 1975, a confrontation took place outside the Church of Notre Dame de la Delivrance in the predominantly Maronite district of Ain el-Rammaneh in East Beirut. A group of armed Palestine Liberation Organization (PLO) guerrillas clashed with a squad of Phalangist Party's Kataeb Regulatory Forces (KRF) militiamen who were diverting traffic for a family baptism at the newly consecrated church. The altercation resulted in the accidental death of the PLO driver after he was shot.

This incident was followed by a dramatic event later that morning. As the congregation gathered outside the church after the ceremony, a group of unidentified gunmen in civilian cars affiliated with the Popular Front for the Liberation of Palestine (PFLP), a PLO faction, opened fire on the church and present VIPs, resulting in the deaths of four individuals, including an off-duty Phalange militant and three bodyguards.

The attack led to escalated tensions as armed Phalangist KRF and NLP Tigers militiamen set up roadblocks in Christian-populated eastern districts, while Palestinian factions did the same in mainly Muslim western sectors of the Lebanese capital. Believing the attackers to be Palestinian guerrillas seeking retaliation, the Phalangists swiftly planned a response.

In a tragic turn of events, a PLO bus passing through Ain el-Rammaneh was ambushed by Phalangist KRF militiamen outside the same church, resulting in the deaths of 27 passengers and injuring 19 others. This escalated the already volatile situation, leading to further unrest and violence in the area.

Efforts to make peace, including intervention by the UAR Secretary General, Mahmoud Ryad, were unsuccessful, and the situation continued to deteriorate. The resignation of key ministers further destabilized the government, leading to a political deadlock.

In the midst of these developments, Prime Minister Rachid El Soleh resigned, and a military government was appointed, sparking protests and further unrest. Despite subsequent attempts to form a new government, challenges persisted, and the conflict continued to escalate.

Efforts were made to mediate the conflict, including a meeting between Rachid Karameh and Yasser Arafat, sponsored by the Syrian delegate to Lebanon. However, these initiatives were unable to quell the unrest, as the country plunged into a new phase of violence and turmoil.

The conflict extended to Beirut and Tripoli, resulting in a significant loss of life and widespread suffering. Civilians were not spared, as they were targeted and killed based on their religious identification. Despite attempts at reconciliation and the establishment of a National Dialogue committee, the violence persisted, with the dispute centering on security and political reforms.

Karameh's refusal to mobilize the military, coupled with ongoing political disagreements, contributed to the escalation of the war, resulting in further loss of life and devastation. These events occurred amidst regional developments, including the signing of the Sinai 2 agreement between Egypt and Israel.

The situation reached a breaking point with the tragic events of "Black Saturday," as Phalanges gunmen perpetrated a massacre in East Beirut, leading to the outbreak of the Hotels War that engulfed Lebanon in turmoil and conflict in 1975.

Country in Turmoil

Lebanon experienced an unprecedented absence of New Year celebrations, as escalating violence led to intense battles in the Hotels War. The conflict saw the Joint Palestinians-Lebanese Forces achieving successive victories amid fierce warfare.

In East Beirut, the Right Forces surrounded densely populated Muslim and Palestinian regions, particularly the refugee camps, citing security concerns and restrictions on movement in the area. They launched a wide-ranging assault on the El Maslakh-Karantina region, predominantly inhabited by lower-class Muslims and Palestinians, many of whom were affiliated with the socialist party led by Kamal Joumblat. In response, the Palestinians and the Lebanese Left attacked the Christian town of Damour, prompting a mass exodus of Christians to President Kamil Chamoun's Palace in Sa'dayat.

The conflict intensified as both the Phalangist and free Nationalists Parties invaded the El Maslakh-Karantina regions, leading to devastating massacres. The Joint Forces retaliated by invading Damour, resulting in further loss of life and widespread looting. Amid these events, Syria intervened directly for the first time by bringing forces of the Palestinian Liberation Army into Lebanon, exacerbating the already dire situation.

As the conflict escalated, various political and military maneuvers took place, including the birth of the Freedom and Human Front on the Christian front and the formation of Lebanon's Arab Army. The situation was further complicated by looting activities carried out by different factions, including the raid of the banks area and the Harbor of Beirut. The political landscape witnessed resistance to proposed reforms, with the Left rejecting the Constitutional Act drafted in Damascus.

The state of affairs deteriorated significantly, with increasing calls for President Franjieh's resignation and violent confrontations that forced him to leave the Presidential Palace. The conflict also saw the loss of civilian lives, including the tragic death of Kamal Joumblat's sister, Linda El Atrash, further fueling the turmoil.

The evolving conflict highlighted the entanglement of regional and international interests, culminating in a devastating civil war with severe implications for the people of Lebanon.

Syria Enters the Lebanese Civil War

The situation in Lebanon escalated rapidly as regional and international factors began to play a crucial role in the country's developments. The Lebanese Phalanges Party and its allies on the right started receiving direct support from Israel, adding significant complexity to the situation.

On April 10th, the Lebanese Parliament made amendments to the country's constitution, allowing for the immediate election of a new president. This was part of a Syrian-led initiative to enable President Franjieh to complete his term while electing his successor before scheduled elections. However, the National Movement rejected this plan, demanding Franjieh's immediate resignation as the president had become aligned with the Lebanese Rights Bloc Staff. The issue of the presidential election caused further friction, as Syria objected to one of the leading candidates who enjoyed strong support from the Muslim community. Despite these challenges, the Syrian-Lebanese Right alliance easily agreed on a presidential candidate.

Meanwhile, Kamal Joumblat and the Lebanese National Movement sought to postpone the elections, but they were ultimately held, resulting in the election of Suki with alleged support from Yasser Arafat. The defeated presidential candidate Raymond Eddé faced a second assassination attempt, which he attributed to the Phalanges. This attempt further exacerbated the tensions between different factions within Lebanon.

The conflict then spread to the mountains and interior regions, posing a significant threat to the Christian community. President-elect Sarkis attempted to build trust and internal harmony by reaching out to Muslim leaders. However, these efforts were overshadowed by the entrance of Syrian forces into Lebanon on June 1st, 1976, which halted the joint forces' advance.

The Syrian intervention was met with resistance from various quarters, leading to fights between different factions in Beirut. The situation deteriorated to the extent that the US and UK had to evacuate their citizens from Lebanon under the protection of the PLO, which had emerged as a key party in the conflict.

The devastating siege of Tal El Za'tar camp, which lasted 52 days, resulted in widespread atrocities and loss of life. Despite Arab efforts to end the war through diplomatic meetings, the conflict continued unabated. Elias Sarkis took the Presidential oath under the protection of Syrian forces, while a significant portion of deputies boycotted the session, reflecting the deep divisions within the country.

The conflict reached a critical juncture, with the Syrian army launching a fierce assault alongside the Lebanese Forces. Arab states moved to prevent a Syrian-PLO defeat, leading to a peace summit in Riyadh and eventually paving the way for Egyptian-Syrian reconciliation.

Tensions between the Lebanese Right and Syria continued, with the Right's collaboration with Israel in South Lebanon adding another layer of complexity to the conflict. The Arab League's decision to form the Arab Prevention Forces and exclude Syria and Lebanon as neutral parties reflected the escalating regional dynamics.

The two-year conflict, often referred to as the Christian Palestinian Conflict, was perceived to have ended with the Syrian solution and Arab cover, leading to the Lebanese Civil War being dubbed the "two-year war."

The Fire Spreads

Arab efforts to establish peace were initiated through the Riyadh and Cairo summits. Subsequently, a quadripartite committee, formed as a result of these gatherings, convened in Beirut with the aim of implementing the 1969 Cairo agreement. The primary objectives were the disarmament of various factions, yet conflict soon ensued.

Syria emerged as a key player in the Lebanese arena. Following a closed meeting of Lebanese bloc leaders, a declaration was made emphasizing the need to liberate Lebanese territories and disperse Palestinian residents in Lebanon among Arab states. Kamal Joumblat, realizing that a decision had been made without his involvement, recognized the potential consequences of his staunch opposition to Damascus and his discussions about the Alawi influence within the Syrian government.

The assassination of the National Movement leader, Kamal Joumblat, on March 16th at his stronghold in the Chouf mountains near a Syrian checkpoint guarded by the Arab Deterrence Forces, incited fury among the Druze. This led to the killing of approximately 200 Christians residing in Chouf, sparking Walid Joumblat to assume the symbolic leadership role of the Druze Confession. While the situation in Beirut somewhat stabilized, tensions flared in the South, resulting in confrontations between Palestinians and the Lebanese Right. Furthermore, conflict intensified between the Palestinians and the Muslims in the South due to the latter's discontent with the behavior and provocation of the Fedayeen. The hope for an end to the war began to dwindle, as both sides continued to train fighters.

Damascus urged the National Movement parties that remained opposed to its intervention to accept the resolutions reached during the two Arab summits.

The visit of Egyptian President Anwar El Sadat to Jerusalem and the prospects of the Camp David agreement became pivotal moments in the conflict on Lebanese soil, leading President Sarkis to recognize the significance of the visit.

A political and strategic reassessment by Syria resulted in a rekindled understanding with the Palestinians, establishing yesterday's adversary as today's ally. The Syrian Foreign Minister denounced the relationship cultivated by Phalanges leader Pierre El-Jemayel with Damascus as a mere ploy.

Simultaneously, signs of discord within the Lebanese Right Bloc began to surface, primarily concerning the Syrian role in Lebanon. Former President Soulayman Franjieh, a member of the Bloc, continued to advocate for the Syrian role. Tensions escalated between Franjieh's supporters and Phalanges partisans in the North, which served as Franjieh's stronghold.

A faction within the Right Bloc emerged, favoring amicable relations with Israel at the expense of their ties with Syria.

At the conclusion of the year, US Secretary of State Sirius Vence's visit to the region, including Lebanon, offered a glimmer of hope. However, his Lebanese counterpart remained pessimistic about any positive impact on the region.

On February 7th, 1978, a clash erupted between Syrian soldiers and Lebanese soldiers at the Fiyadieh barracks in East Beirut, resulting in the deaths of over 30 individuals, predominantly Syrian soldiers. President Al Assad vehemently condemned the incident, describing it as a trap and a massacre. President Sarkis dispatched his Foreign Minister to Damascus to alleviate the escalating tensions.

Eventually, El Assad retracted his demand for a military trial against the Lebanese soldiers in exchange for a statement from the Lebanese Bloc affirming its unwavering trust in Syrian policy. However, this did little to alleviate the strain between the Lebanese Right and Syria, with recurrent clashes between the two sides persisting. The situation deteriorated in the South, culminating in March of that year when Israeli forces launched the Litani Project, invading and occupying Lebanese territories up to the Litani River.

The International Security Council implemented Resolution 425, demanding Israel's withdrawal from Lebanon and the dispatch of international forces to oversee the withdrawal. Although Israeli forces began to withdraw, they ceded significant portions of the occupied regions to Major Sa'd Haddad to establish a so-called security belt and the Army of South Lebanon militia. Claims arose that the international forces were allegedly providing cover for Palestinians, leading to confrontations between Palestinians and the UN forces, resulting in casualties and damage to the representatives of the international community in Lebanon.

Tensions flared in the summer of that year when Bachir El-Jemayel, leader of the Lebanese Forces militia, dispatched units under the command of Samir Geageaa to raid the northern town of Ehden, a stronghold of the Franjieh family. This led to a brutal massacre in which Toni Franjieh, the son of former President Soulayman Franjieh, his wife, their 2 and a half-year-old daughter, and over 30 of his supporters were killed. Members close to Bachir El-Jemayel from the Phalanges assert that the operation did not intend to culminate in a massacre.Accusations and Conflicts in Lebanon

The Phalanges Party has leveled accusations against the Syrian Forces, claiming that they are seeking revenge on Christian civilians in response to Franjieh's murder.

Tensions escalated in early July as clashes erupted between Syrian and Lebanese Forces militias, leading to violent bombings of East Beirut by the Syrian Army. Relations deteriorated between Damascus and President Sarkis, the nominal high commander of the Arab Prevention Forces, after he broke his silence and declared that President El Assad had ordered the APF to cease-fire. Sarkis initially submitted his resignation, only to withdraw it a few days later.

The bombing of East Beirut persisted, and the Lebanese President accused both the Phalanges and the Syrians of bombing the Presidential palace, an accusation that both sides vehemently denied. Amidst this turmoil, M. MOUSA El-Sader, head of the Supreme Shiite Islamic Council, disappeared after returning to Lebanon from a visit to Damascus, and doubts surfaced about the involvement of Libya and certain Palestinian factions in his disappearance.

The Amal Movement asserted that the Palestinians and Libyans played a role in the Imam's disappearance. Against the backdrop of the ongoing conflict between Damascus and the Lebanese Right, the International Council issued a resolution on October 6th calling for an end to the bombing of East Beirut without explicitly naming Syria.

Around 10 days later, the Beit El-dinh meeting took place, where the foreign Ministers of the Arab States supporting the APF convened. With Saudi Arabia's assistance, President Sarkis managed to persuade Damascus to withdraw the Syrian Forces from Achrafieh, replacing them with Saudi and Sudanese Forces. This development led to the resolution of the protracted conflict between Syria and Christians and a thawing of relations between Presidents El-Assad and Sarkis.

In January 1979, the PLO suffered a significant setback when Israel assassinated Ali Hassan Salamah, also known as Abou Hassan, who was in charge of Yasser Arafat's Security. Bachir El-Jemayel made efforts to warn Salamah of the danger to his life shortly before the assassination through an emissary he sent to one of his supporters.

Lebanon appeared to be heavily influenced by regional developments, with fluctuating peace and ongoing conflict. Saudi Forces withdrew from the APF, and other Arab detachments followed suit. In Teheran, the first Islamic Iranian government ordered the Iranian detachment working with the UN Forces to return. Members of the National Movement Staff accused Arab States of conspiring against them.

The Lebanese government sought to strengthen the Army and deployed it to the South, where it faced opposition from Palestinian and Lebanese left factions, as well as attacks from the Army of south Lebanon under Sa'd Haddad's command. Haddad declared the establishment of the Free Lebanese State due to the perceived Syrian and Palestinian occupation of the country.

A new phase of the Lebanese War began, marked by targeting innocent citizens through booby-trapped cars and bombs. One such attempt on the life of Lebanese Forces militia leader Bachir El-Jemayel led to the tragic death of his

18-month-old daughter. On July 7th, 1980, Bachir El-Jemayel decisively defeated the Free Nationalist's Noumour militias after ferocious battles, solidifying his position as the sole leader of the Lebanese Right.

Bachir emerged as a key figure in a country at a standstill, poised to embark on a new endeavor, drawing inspiration from his Israeli allies.

The Rising New Parties

In the late 1970s and early 1980s, Lebanon became a battleground as Syrian, Palestinian, and Israeli forces, along with various Lebanese militias, vied for power and influence.

President Sarkis attempted to mobilize the Lebanese Army, but his efforts were not taken seriously. Meanwhile, Walid Joumblat distanced himself from the National Movement, previously led by his late father, and instead focused on strengthening the military force of the Socialist Progressive Party's Druze-majority militia.

The conflict between Iraq and Iran spilled over into Lebanon, resulting in attacks on each other's services and embassies. This bloody series culminated in an attack on the Iraqi Embassy, leaving many dead or wounded.

In the southern region of Lebanon, UN forces aimed to build trust with the local population but faced harsh military realities.

Tensions rose between President Sarkis and Prime Minister Selim El-Hoss, leading to a deadlock. A new government, headed by Chafiq El-Wazzan, was subsequently formed.

The involvement of Syria and Israel grew as the Lebanese Forces militia constructed a road from their control areas in the Kesserwan Mountains UA to Beka', towards Zahleh city. The Lebanese Christian leader, Bachir El-Jemayel, believed that the Beka' and mountain Christians should not be separated. The complex relationship with Israel, seen as a means to counter Palestinians and Syrians, was further complicated by Syria's control of the Lebanese Beka' Valley.

As tensions escalated, Bachir El-Jemayel sought Israeli intervention, prompting the Israeli Air Force to down two Syrian helicopters. In response, President El-Assad deployed SAM 6 antiaircraft missiles into the Beka' Valley, leading to air battles in Lebanese skies.

This escalation caused a breach of the Red-Lines Agreement between Israel and Syria, leading to increased verbal confrontations. Efforts to find a settlement were initiated by diplomats Philip Habib and Maurice Draper, with ongoing verbal sparring between both sides.

In the midst of these events, acts of terrorism targeting civilians occurred, including bombings in cinemas.

Meanwhile, the Saudi crown prince introduced the ME Peace Project.

On September 4th, 1981, the French ambassador to Lebanon, Louis De Lamarre, was assassinated in West Beirut, adding to the turmoil. The Zahleh crisis finally ended after three months, with the withdrawal of the Lebanese Forces' militia and the deployment of Lebanese Security Forces.

Philip Habib successfully mediated, leading to the retention of Syrian missiles in the Beka' Valley.

In a separate development, a violent exchange between the PLO and the Israeli Army on the Lebanese-Israeli border heightened tension. After further mediation by Habib, a ceasefire agreement was reached, which the PLO considered a victory.

Israel perceived the ceasefire agreement as a new threat due to the growing political influence of the PLO, leading to increased infiltration efforts by Israel.

As these events unfolded, the Amal Movement emerged as a significant force in southern Lebanon, engaging in fierce battles with various Palestinian groups and weakening Baghdad-backed organizations. The growing authority of the Amal Movement led to serious consideration of its role in decision-making in Beirut.

In early 1982, Yasser Arafat led a parade to showcase the strength of his organization, conscious that it might be their last in Lebanon given the escalating conflict in the region.

Israel Invades

On June 4th, 1982, the Israeli invasion of Lebanon commenced with intense Israeli Air Force raids on West Beirut and the South. The invasion was sparked by an assassination attempt on the Israeli ambassador in London, Shlomo Argov, even though his attackers were from Abou Nidal's group, affiliated with Yasser Arafat. Israel deployed twice the forces used in the '73 war against Egypt and Syria. Two days after the air raids, land invasion of Lebanese territories began.

There was an expectation that the Israeli Forces would push PLO Forces 40 km away from the border to avoid the impact of PLO missiles. The US Secretary of State Alexander Hague swiftly supported the Israeli air raids and seemed to align with the ideas of Israeli Defense Minister Ariel Sharon.

Although the Israeli Government had agreed on a 40km invasion, Minister Ariel Sharon had different plans, influenced by Bachir's insistence that the invasion must reach Beirut.

As the Israeli Forces advanced towards Beirut from various points, the Palestinians initially fell back, but fierce resistance from the Golan brigade and Palestinian refugee camps in the South stalled the invasion for several days. The camps were left devastated. Despite PLO's retreat, criticism persisted.

In the early days of the invasion, Syria, like other world capitals, initially believed the Israeli operation would be limited. However, as the Israeli procession neared the strategic depth of Syrian territories, fierce fighting erupted in the Beka'a, resulting in severe losses for the Israeli Army.

The invasion witnessed significant aerial warfare. US delegate Philip Habib returned to the region to arrange a cease-fire between Syria and Israel. President El Assad's anger led Damascus to declare it would never again receive Habib.

As the siege of West Beirut tightened and Israeli troops entered Chouf Mountain without resistance, the city faced relentless bombardment. Negotiations commenced for the Palestinians to pull out from Beirut.

At the Lebanese level, President Sarkis called for the withdrawal of all foreign armies from Lebanon, including the Syrian and Palestinian forces. The National Rescue Organization was established, encompassing key figures such as Bachir El Jemayel, Amal movement leader Nabih Berri, and Socialist Progressive Party Leader Walid Joumblat.

In Washington, Alexander Hague faced growing pressure as rifts within the US Administration emerged. East Beirut welcomed the invading troops, while Right Leaders attempted to maintain political and military distance from the invasion.

During the invasion, Phalanges Party Leader Sheik Pierre El Jemayel expressed reservations about relations with Israel, distinct from his son Bachir, evident in an interview with Israeli television at the time.

The devastation and encirclement of West Beirut continued for several weeks, with negotiations ongoing to evacuate the Palestinians. However, the battle had only just begun.

Arab Capital is Down

Israel's Defense Minister, Ariel Sharon, achieved his long-sought goal when he set foot in an Arab capital for the first time. His forces encircled West Beirut, subjecting it to a relentless siege and bombardment. Israeli Air Force planes intermittently dropped leaflets urging the population to evacuate the capital before facing renewed destructive attacks.

Although there had been a wave of emigration from the besieged city, approximately 300 thousand people remained in West Beirut. The Palestinian command had decided to withdraw, but they sought the most favorable terms before agreeing to the withdrawal. The Lebanese Left Leaderships held differing positions, with some urging the Palestinians to be realistic, while others fought to secure the best possible terms.

To intensify the pressure, Israeli Forces, assisted by Lebanese Forces militias, cut off the water supply to West Beirut. US delegate Philip Habib was visibly angered, expressing his frustration during a telephone call with Washington. However, the siege faced various challenges.

Despite reaching several cease-fires while political negotiations aimed to remove the Palestinians, these were consistently broken, with Habib accusing Sharon of violating them.

Efforts by the Palestinians and the Left to garner international support, particularly from essential ally, the Soviet Union, were met with indifference from Moscow.

The violent bombardment of West Beirut continued, with Ariel Sharon's troops using internationally banned weapons such as cluster and phosphorous bombs. A devastating new weapon, a vacuum bomb, was used for the first time against civilians, causing widespread destruction and loss of life.

Alleging that their target was Yasser Arafat, who was in the building when it was struck, Israel made repeated desperate attempts to assassinate the PLO leader.

Meanwhile, Bachir El-Jemayel's bid for the presidency faced opposition from Syria, with his opponents using his associations with Israeli Defense Minister Ariel Sharon to undermine his candidacy. Nevertheless, many believed that Bachir had matured politically and was the best candidate to control the situation in Lebanon.

Bachir El-Jemayel made significant efforts, including seeking the support of his adversaries for his candidacy, with the intervention of Speaker of the Parliament Kamel El-Asa'ad in some cases.

On August 23rd, the Lebanese presidential election was held under the protection of Israeli forces, marking a shift from the previous Syrian-backed elections 6 years earlier. Bachir El-Jemayel was elected as the country's president after significant difficulty in reaching a quorum.

Following Bachir's election, a meeting with Menah Begin in Nahariya, Israel, was reported to be very challenging. However, negotiations conducted by Washington to remove the PLO from Beirut were making progress, despite initial refusals from some Arab States to receive the Palestinian fighters.

Though the negotiations progressed, the worst Israeli bombardments of West Beirut and the Beka'a took place. Sharon faced not only resistance from the Joint Lebanese-Palestinian Forces but also increasing objections within the Israeli government and rising protest among Israeli troops.

Eventually, an agreement was reached for the PLO and the 85th Syrian brigade to withdraw from Beirut in exchange for the placement of multinational forces from the USA, France, Britain, and Italy in Beirut, along with US commitment to protect Palestinian refugees.

The multinational forces were present for only 2 weeks when the US President declared the end of their mission, despite an initial plan for them to stay for at least a month.

Just three weeks after Bachir El-Jemayel's election as president, a massive explosion at the Phalanges' headquarters in Achrafieh resulted in his death and the deaths of many others. This event shattered the hopes of thousands of Lebanese, while reigniting hope for others.

The circumstances of Bachir El-Jemayel's death led to widespread speculation, and a funeral was held for the President-elect with attendees ranging from allies to adversaries, all seeking to understand the situation and its implications.

The Israeli troops swiftly advanced and overcame the resilient resistance in West Beirut, prompting accusations of causing further civilian casualties.

The National Movement parties' fighters bravely stood up to the invading troops, risking their lives despite knowing they were likely to lose.

The birth of the Lebanese National Resistance troops was announced by the Secretary General of the Lebanese Communist Party and the communist Activity Organization, with operations led by Maronite Christian Elias Atallah. The resistance achieved multiple successful operations against the occupation Army.

Eventually, the Israeli troops withdrew, bringing an end to Beirut's occupation, and West Beirut was free once more.

The Bloodshed

Bachir El-Jemayel's assassination dealt a devastating blow to the aspirations of the Lebanese Right and Israel. Israel understood that the call for revenge from the Right was more than just rhetoric. In response to the President-elect's assassination, Washington's representative Maurice Draper traveled to Israel to meet with chief of staff Raphael Etan following the Israeli Army's invasion of West Beirut. Etan sensed a strong desire for retaliation during his meeting with the leader of the Lebanese Forces militia.

Initially, Washington had pledged to safeguard the Palestinian refugees after the PLO's departure from Beirut. However, the premature withdrawal of the Multinational Troops left the Palestinians vulnerable. Plans to breach the Sabra and Shatila Camp began with a war council meeting involving the Lebanese Forces militia.

A crucial account of these events is found in a speech delivered by Ariel Sharon at the Israeli Synagogue addressing the massacre. Sharon revealed that on Wednesday, September 15th, the Israeli general Amir Dolori met with the Phalangist commander and Col. Michel Aoun, the head of Lebanese Army units in Beirut. During the meeting, the northern commander urged the Lebanese colonel to persuade the government to allow the entry of the Lebanese army into the camps. However, the government refused Israel's request, and Col. Aoun informed the Israelis that he was under orders to fire at the Israeli Army.

On Thursday at 6:00 pm on September 16th, 1982, the Israeli Army brought over 300 militants of the Lebanese Forces into Sabra and Shatila Camp in an operation purportedly aimed at clearing the camp of approximately 2,000 Palestinian fighters left by Yasser Arafat. This assertion was entirely false. The massacre persisted until 8 am on Saturday, September 18th, for over 36 hours.

The camp's inhabitants soon became aware that something horrific was unfolding. The perpetrators, growing impatient, fired shots that reverberated alongside the screams, mingling with the smell of gunpowder and blood. The camp was consumed by an atmosphere of terror and surrealism. Members of the Lebanese Forces began gathering women and children, and even infants fell victim to the massacre.

At Sabra and Shatila, dignity was desecrated. Despite sustaining multiple gunshot wounds, one of Maher's sisters lay on the ground, unable to move. The assailants started moving women and children out of the camp toward the stadium, where a dreadful surprise awaited. As for Souad's tragedy, it did not conclude with the violation that took place in her own home.

Elie Hobeika, Head of Security of the Lebanese Forces militia, was the primary Lebanese figure accused of responsibility for the massacre. Michel Samaha was one of Hobeika's closest political allies; he knew and worked closely with him.

After the details of the events in Sabra and Shatila were revealed, 400,000 Israelis took to the streets in protest against their country's involvement in the massacre. Maurice Draper sent a verbal message to Ariel Sharon, commencing with a scathing rebuke and continuing to express his dismay.

Faced with public pressure, the Israeli Government established the Cahan Commission to investigate the massacre. The inquiry revealed that the Israeli Army was aware of civilians being killed within the camp.

No fewer than 800 individuals lost their lives in the massacre at Sabra and Shatila..

The Retreat

Following the Sabra and Shatila massacre, Israeli troops withdrew from West Beirut. Soon after, the multinational forces swiftly returned to Lebanon. In the midst of this turmoil, the Lebanese parliament elected Amine El-Jemayel as President following the tragic death of his younger brother, President-elect Bachir El-Jemayel. Meanwhile, former president Kamil Chamoun initially vied for the presidency, but ultimately withdrew his candidacy due to significant pressure from Washington, paving the way for Amine's ascension.

As President El-Jemayel declared Beirut an open city, signaling a potential end to Lebanon's war, the Lebanese Army's deployment in Beirut was initially met with approval from the city's inhabitants. However, allegations soon surfaced, with citizens and political parties on the western side of the capital accusing the Army of initiating a series of arrests. Despite the efforts of the prisoners' mothers to protest, their voices went unheard.

Simultaneously, diplomatic efforts were underway in Washington to broker an agreement between Lebanon and Israel in order to end their state of hostility and facilitate the withdrawal of Israeli troops from Lebanon. Recognizing the urgency, Washington pushed forward with the negotiations, contending not only with Syrian opposition and Soviet support, but also with escalating hostilities within Lebanon itself.

The situation in Mount Lebanon took a concerning turn as civilian casualties mounted due to clashes between the Lebanese Forces militia of Christian majority and the Socialist Progressive Party's militia of Druze majority led by Walid Joumblat. The Lebanese Army's attempts to deploy in Mount Lebanon, which was still occupied by the Israeli Army, highlighted the complexities and challenges facing the country. The escalating blows exchanged between the Resistance members and the Israeli occupation Army only served to further complicate matters.

In a separate incident, an enormous explosion destroyed the Israeli Army's outpost in Tyre-South Lebanon, resulting in the deaths of numerous Israeli soldiers and Lebanese Palestinian prisoners. These events shattered the expectations of those who had orchestrated the invasion and underscored the brutal realities of the Lebanese war.

Subsequently, an attempt on the life of Socialist Progressive Party Leader Walid Joumblat in West Beirut further fueled tensions. Joumblat attributed the incident to the conflict in Mount Lebanon and held the Lebanese president responsible, a claim that was denied by Amine El-Jemayel.

Amidst these tumultuous events, a devastating blow was dealt when a booby-trapped car targeted the American Embassy in Beirut, claiming the lives of over 60 individuals, including senior CIA officers who were convening for a regional meeting. Despite this tragedy, President Reagan reaffirmed his country's unwavering commitment to pursuing peaceful efforts and promptly dispatched Secretary of State Shultz to Beirut to reiterate America's support for President El-Jemayel.

As the Lebanese-Israeli negotiations drew to a close, Secretary Shultz journeyed to Damascus, marking a pivotal moment in the region's political landscape. A month later, Lebanon and Israel signed the 17th of May agreement, signaling a significant diplomatic milestone. Meanwhile, tensions between Syrian President Hafez El-Assad and PLO leader Yasser Arafat reached a boiling point, leading to a bitter conflict within the PLO and culminating in Arafat's assassination in the Beka'a Valley.

In a surprising turn of events, Yasser Arafat reemerged in Tripoli, months after his departure from Lebanon. His subsequent journey to Damascus, which some perceived as a reconciliation effort with Syria, was overshadowed by the internal challenges within his organization. Arafat's declaration of the expulsion of the secessionists and Damascus's subsequent expulsion of Arafat marked a tumultuous period, culminating in Arafat's accusation that

Damascus had orchestrated an attempt on his life. In the midst of the tumultuous events in Lebanon, Syria's allies formed the National Rescue Front, with key figures such as Walid Joumblat, former President Soulayman Franjieh, and former Prime Minister Rachid Karameh joining forces. Amidst this, questions arose regarding the absence of Nabih Berreh, the leader of the Amal Movement. Tensions flared as clashes erupted between anti-government Lebanese factions and the Lebanese Army in Beirut. Despite the turmoil, the Army managed to regain control, signaling the deteriorating political and military climate in the region. Notably, Israel chose to withdraw from the Chouf mountains, facing resistance from some Christian groups who sought to dissuade the Israeli military from this action.

Violent confrontations unfolded in the Chouf Mountains between Druze and Christian groups, with Israel arming both sides before retreating south. This conflict escalated, leading to a fierce battle between the Lebanese forces militia and the socialist progressive party. As war erupted on multiple fronts, the Lebanese Army engaged in intense battles against the Socialist Progressive Party, which had the backing of Palestinian troops and leftist factions.

The outcome was grim for the Christian fighters, as control was ceded to the Socialist Progressive Party. Hundreds of Christians were besieged in Deir El-Kamar town, enduring atrocities and massacres in Mount Lebanon. Additionally, the Socialist Progressive Party alleged discovering massacres committed by the Lebanese Forces militias during their control over various regions in the Mountain.

The multinational forces threw their support behind the Lebanese government, becoming embroiled in the conflict. This involvement came at a cost, with Washington paying a heavy price for its role in the war in Lebanon. The devastating truck bombing at the U.S. Marines headquarters near Beirut's international Airport, which claimed the lives of 241 marines, marked a significant blow to Washington.

Meanwhile, the Islamic Jihad claimed responsibility for this attack and another aimed at the French paratrooper's headquarters, sparking concerns about an Iranian role. The Syrian President, seizing the opportunity, dealt a severe blow to his adversaries. The resistance against Israeli military posts continued, with the Syrian Air Defense downing both Israeli and American aircraft, shaking Washington and leading to Soviet involvement in the conflict.

Lebanon was engulfed in turmoil, with Yasser Arafat engaging in a bloody battle in Tripoli, facing bombardment from Syrian and Israeli forces. Amid this chaos, Arafat was forced to leave Lebanon for the second time, with no immediate plans to return.

As the conflict progressed, President El-Assad maneuvered to deliver a significant blow to the U.S. and President El-Jemayel, while the Amal Movement was set to assume a major role in Lebanon. The 6th of February Intifada marked a decisive and sweeping attack by West Beirut parties against the Lebanese Army, ultimately resulting in the dispersion of the army and the withdrawal of the multinational forces.

In the end, President El-Assad emerged victorious, gaining control over Lebanon. However, the conclusion of this long and arduous conflict only hinted at the beginning of new challenges, as chaos lurked around the corner for the embattled country.

Rivalries

In 1984, Lebanon was divided into zones of influence controlled by various militias. In West Beirut, the 6th of February Upheaval resulted in the President's authority collapsing, and control was shared among the Amal movement, The Socialist Progressive Party, The Lebanese Communist Party, the Murabitoon Movement, and other smaller groups. Meanwhile in East Beirut, the Lebanese Forces militia and some brigades of the Lebanese Army, loyal to either President El-Jemayel or the Lebanese Forces, held dominance. President El-Jemayel, realizing the significance of involving Syria, traveled there to meet with President Hafez El-Assad. Subsequently, national reconciliation conferences in Geneva and Lausanne involving Saudi Arabia and Syria were held, although political reform remained a significant obstacle.

Efforts towards peace in Lebanon were initiated by Emir Bandar Ben Sultan and Rafik El-Hariri, a Saudi of Lebanese origin, under the auspices of the Kingdom of Saudi Arabia. In West Beirut, ongoing battles aimed at gaining control of residential areas ensued for several years.

Following the Lausanne Conference, a battle in West Beirut led by the Socialist Progressive Party militias and the Murabitoon resulted in a ceasefire after causing numerous casualties. In the south, the death of Major Sa'd Haddad led to Major General Antoine Lahed assuming command of the Southern Lebanese Army Militia working with Israel. Pressure from Syria prompted President El-Jemayel to revoke the 17th of May Agreement, leading to the formation of a government of National Unity with Rachid Karameh at the helm.

At the same time, the Lebanese Government closed the Israeli liaison office in Lebanon. Attacks on American interests persisted, and the year ended with no resolution in sight for the war in Lebanon.

The resistance in the South continued to challenge the occupation forces, leading to the birth of the National Resistance and Islamic Resistance. Israeli-Lebanese military talks commenced, but Israel initiated a withdrawal before a security agreement was reached, continuing its "Iron Fist Policy."

The policy involved besieging and penetrating southern villages, leading to tragic consequences, such as the bombing in Ma'raka and the siege in Zrariah. Additionally, a series of kidnappings commenced in Beirut, including the abduction of William Buckley, the CIA Station Manager in Lebanon, who tragically died under torture.

In Tripoli, the Islamic Tawhid Movement engaged in a bloody war against Lebanese and Alawi militias allied to Syria. Additionally, internal conflicts within the Phalanges Party and a coup attempt added to the complexity of Lebanon's political landscape.Protecting the Christian Community in a Time of Crisis

Amidst the turmoil, leaders asserted that their actions were aimed at safeguarding the Christian Community and maintaining autonomy from Syrian influence. President El-Jemayel, originally slated to attend the funeral of Soviet leader Constantine Chernenko, altered his plans in response to the crisis. Choosing to prioritize the situation at hand, he engaged with key Christian figures in an effort to reconcile matters. Despite opposition to the upheaval from Washington, the President declined a proposal for assistance from Syria, and found himself without direct support.

In a fiery spring season, the Lebanese forces militia faced the imminent loss of their final strongholds in regions under Muslim and Leftist control, particularly in East Tyre where intense confrontations unfolded. Following the withdrawal of Christian fighters, a wave of vengeance targeted those who remained in the area. Accusations of atrocities committed by the Lebanese Forces militia during their occupation emerged from Islamic and Leftist militias.

In April, Walid Joumblat and Nabih Berreh journeyed to Damascus, only to return a few hours later before the allied militias of Amal Movement, the Socialist Progressive Party, and the Communist Party suppressed the Murabitoon Movement.

The early days of summer saw the Amal Movement launching an attack on Palestinian refugee camps in Beirut, claiming to be dismantling what they labeled the "Arafat way," while the Palestinians saw their actions as a struggle for survival. This marked the beginning of the Camps War, a conflict that raged for three years and resulted in numerous casualties. Later in the year, Shiite militants commandeered a Jordanian plane and demanded the expulsion of Palestinian combatants from the refugee camps. Despite releasing the passengers shortly before the set detonation time, they ultimately destroyed the aircraft. The Beirut Airport bore witness to several hijackings, including that of the American TWA plane, during which the hijackers sought the release of 700 Lebanese individuals captured by Israel and tragically killed an American marine.

West Beirut erupted in violence as militias from the Socialist Progressive Party and Amal Movement clashed in what became known as the Flay War, sparked by an attempt by the Socialist Progressive Party to replace the Lebanese flag with their own on governmental buildings. Countless innocent lives were lost in these battles.

In Tripoli, Sheikh Sa'id Sha'ban accused Syria of preparing to perpetrate a massacre, while Damascus advocates argued against the strict Islamic faction's occupation of the city.

Partisans of the Islamic Tawhid Movement kidnapped four Soviet diplomats in an effort to pressure Moscow into influencing Damascus. Tragically, one diplomat was killed, and the bodies of the others were mutilated upon their release after the Islamists were killed.

Ultimately, following a six-day onslaught by Lebanese militias allied with Damascus and supported by Syrian artillery and tanks, the Tawhid Movement capitulated, allowing Syrian troops to enter the capital of North Lebanon.

In East Beirut, a series of developments unfolded, culminating in Hobeika and Geageaa's upheaval in March. Efforts were made to broker an understanding with Syria, exacerbating divisions within the Christian community. President El-Jemayel sought a written authorization from the highest echelons of the Lebanese Forces militia, Samir Geagea and Elie Hobeika, to negotiate with Syria.

However, on May 9th, Hobeika staged a counter-coup within the Lebanese Forces, declaring Lebanon's allegiance to the Arab world and asserting Syria's special role in its future. Notably, a Lebanese forces militia leader visited Damascus for the first time in a decade, marking a significant shift. With Syria's escalating influence in Lebanon, efforts were made to broker a tripartite agreement to end the war. Rafik El-Hariri played a crucial role behind the scenes.

Karim Bakradouni's visit to Damascus and meeting with Abdel Halim Khaddam galvanized Maronite Christians to assess the situation, leading to discord within their ranks. In a turn of events, despite initial reluctance, Hobeika, Berreh, and Joumblat signed the Tripartite agreement in Damascus, underlining the complex negotiations at play.

Less than three weeks later, Samir Geagea launched a formidable assault on forces supporting Elie Hobeika, effectively dismantling the Tripartite agreement. The intervention of the Syrian Chief of Staff was necessary to preserve Hobeika's position. Geagea instructed Bakradouni to go to Hobeika. Later, Hobeika attempted to return to East Beirut with backing from Damascus, but the Lebanese Army intervened and successfully defeated Hobeika's forces amidst ongoing clashes between the PLO and the Amal Movement. The Palestinians swiftly raided the Shiite fighters' positions in the strategic town of Maghdousha.

Amal made unsuccessful attempts to reclaim the town, which overlooked crucial southern areas. An agreement was eventually reached, leading to the withdrawal of Palestinian fighters from Maghdousha, which was subsequently taken over by Hezbollah. This move intensified the rivalry between Hezbollah and Amal for leadership within the Shiite community. Militia members across Lebanon imposed protection taxes on shop owners and engaged in coercive practices, while numerous armed individuals were involved in theft, looting, and other illicit activities. Furthermore, the militias supplanted the judicial system. Given the gravity of the situation, intervention was deemed necessary to halt the deterioration, and Beirut once again faced the challenge of confronting armed groups.

Syria is Back

The turbulent streets of West Beirut became a battleground for the destructive whims of armed factions. Despite numerous attempts to broker peace agreements among militia leaders, every ceasefire was short-lived. The leaders acknowledged their inability to control their undisciplined fighters, leading to repeated outbreaks of violence.

Following the Israeli invasion, a new Islamic movement emerged within the Shiite community, with Hezbollah at its forefront. Amid widespread belief that Iran was orchestrating attacks against Western interests and citizens in Lebanon, tensions escalated.

In March 1985, a devastating explosion rocked the predominantly Shiite suburb of Bir-El-'Abed, targeting prominent Shiite figure Mohammed Hussein Fadelallah. Though Fadelallah, often dubbed the spiritual leader of

Hezbollah, denied official ties to the organization, he narrowly survived the attack which claimed the lives of over 80 people and left around 200 injured.

Subsequently, reports surfaced suggesting that the explosion had been orchestrated by American intelligence, financed by Saudi Arabia and carried out by local operatives. These events precipitated a chain of violent incidents.

Hezbollah's ascendancy not only weakened the Amal Movement, the longstanding representative of Lebanese Shiites, but also led to the emergence of an Islamic faction within Amal that eventually defected to join Hezbollah. Ethnic tensions soared in West Beirut as Christians faced kidnappings and displacement, while a spate of abductions targeted Westerners, especially Americans.

Prompted by concerns over Iranian influence in Lebanon, Syria intervened to quell the escalating conflict between Hezbollah and Amal, which raged until the conclusion of the Lebanese War. Amal's involvement in the Camps War against Palestinian forces further stretched its resources, triggering clashes with the socialist-communist alliance in West Beirut. This conflict, ominously dubbed the 6-Day War, left Amal in a dire predicament.

As the crisis reached its peak, the leaders of the city's western districts, alongside Prime Minister Rachid Karameh, implored Syria's intervention to halt the militia infighting. In a bid to stabilize the situation, key figures, including Walid Joumblat and George Hawi, were summoned to Damascus.

The fractious battles coincided with the Camps War, with Amal forces securing victory along the borders of the refugee camps in Beirut, bolstered by Syrian support. As the 6th brigade, which had defected from the Lebanese Army in the turmoil of February 6th, 1984, joined forces with Amal, leftist factions refrained from participation. The Palestinians regarded the conflict as regional rather than solely local, while pursuing tangible gains amidst the violence.

In February 1987, Syrian troops reentered Beirut, after an absence of more than four years. Tensions mounted, as confrontations erupted between Syrian forces and Hezbollah, culminating in the death of 22 Hezbollah militants in one clash.

By May 1987, amid prolonged discord within the government, Prime Minister Rachid Karameh resigned, citing inefficacy and wavering leadership. Despite presenting his resignation to the public, he did not formally tender it to President El-Jemayel, who equally refrained from accepting it. Subsequently, El Jemayel appointed Salim El-Hoss as the acting Prime Minister.

Tragically, on June 1st, while en route to Beirut aboard a Lebanese Army helicopter, Rachid Karameh fell victim to a fatal bomb explosion beneath his seat. Suspicions of collusion involving the Lebanese Army arose immediately. In the aftermath of the war, Samir Geagea, the leader of the Lebanese Forces militia, was convicted of Karameh's assassination.Finally, the long-standing conflict between the militias of Amal and Hezbollah erupted into open warfare known as the Brothers' War. The streets of Beirut's Dahiya El-Janoubiah, predominantly Shiite, and parts of West Beirut became a battleground for the two sides. Hezbollah fighters overran many of Amal Movement's outposts in Dahiya El-Janoubiah, dealing a fatal blow when they captured the Movement's headquarters. The defection of a significant number of Amal militants to join Hezbollah further contributed to the Movement's defeat. Amidst the violence, a women's protest calling for an end to the fighting between "brothers" was met with gunfire, reflecting the desperation of the inhabitants who were weary of the bloodshed and destruction.

In response, Syria swiftly made preparations for its troops to enter Dahiya El-Janoubiah to restore order. During this tumultuous period, the Head of security and Investigation in the Syrian Forces, Brigadier General Ghazi Kana'an, visited Mr. Mohammed Hussein Fadelallah. On his return, Kana'an's convoy was targeted by Hezbollah militants, underscoring the escalating tensions between the militia and the Syrian Army.

The underlying cause of the crisis was the conflicting interests of Iran and Syria in Lebanon. To address this, Iranian and Syrian officials convened to find a resolution. Meanwhile, the conflict shifted from Beirut to the South, the stronghold of the Amal Movement, leading to brutal clashes and numerous casualties. The violence reached a turning point in 1988 when Daoud Daoud, an influential figure in Amal Movement, was assassinated, leading to accusations and suspicions among different factions.

Amidst this turmoil, the Amal Movement lifted its siege on Palestinian forces, only to have Palestinian organizations opposed to Yasser Arafat's rule take their place, resulting in the devastating Camps War, leaving thousands dead and injured.

In the south, the Israeli Occupation Army and its local allies faced a resilient Islamic resistance led by Hezbollah, creating a climate of fear and uncertainty for the occupying forces.

By 1988, the War of Lebanon had entered its 13th year, with over 100,000 lives lost. The conflict showed no signs of abating; instead, it seemed poised to unleash an unprecedented level of destruction on Lebanon.

The Solution Must Come

In the early months of '88, Lebanon found itself at a critical juncture. President Amine El-Jemayel's term was coming to an end, sparking speculation about his successor in accordance with Lebanon's established oral agreement that the president should be a Maronite Christian. The country was abuzz with several Lebanese politicians vying for the presidency, but the decision wasn't solely a local matter. Regional and international factors, particularly the influences of Syria and the United States, had to be taken into consideration.

Negotiations between Lebanon's Christians and Syria, facilitated by the USA, commenced in an attempt to select a new president. Former President Soulayman Franjieh emerged as a candidate with the backing of Damascus, but faced strong opposition from various factions in East Beirut who perceived Syria's hand in the selection process.

Tensions escalated as Parliament members from the East Area boycotted the session regarding the presidential election, amid accusations directed at the Lebanese Army and the Lebanese Forces for obstructing the attendance of East Beirut representatives. Meanwhile, Richard Murphy, Assistant Secretary of State, tirelessly shuttled between Beirut and Damascus in a bid to broker a solution. President El-Jemayel adamantly refused any extension of his term.

As the deadline loomed, President El-Jemayel visited his Syrian counterpart, carrying two propositions: either to agree on a candidate other than El-Daher, acceptable to all parties, or for Damascus to provide assurances to the Christians regarding El-Daher's plans, political platform, and reforms.

Faced with the impending presidential vacancy, President El-Jemayel made the decision to transfer power to a provisional government that would oversee the presidential elections. This move was met with resistance from both Christian and Muslim communities, leading to a precarious situation where the country found itself with two governments.

Efforts to fill the void left by President El-Jemayel's departure from office proved fruitless, with the parliament failing to elect a successor. Tensions continued to escalate, culminating in violent clashes between Lebanese Army units supporting General Aoun and the Lebanese Forces militias.

General Aoun's troops gained ground until a ceasefire was declared.

Amidst this turmoil, the international community took notice, and a six-party committee led by Kuwait's Foreign Minister was formed to broker peace. Lebanon became the focal point once again, and the urgency to find a lasting solution to the country's internal strife became all the more apparent.

Ending the War

Beirut, on both sides, experienced intense shelling that targeted residential areas. Despite several cease-fires reached by the Arab League's committee, the violence persisted. Eventually, General Aoun agreed to lift the siege he had imposed on illegal harbors run by militias, sparking further crisis with his opponents.

In East Beirut, tensions mounted as the Lebanese Forces militia and the Lebanese Army units under Aoun's command prepared for more conflict. Iraq played a significant role in arming both sides, who were opposed to Syria. On May 16, 1989, an enormous explosion rocked West Beirut, killing Sunni leader Mufti Hassan Khaled. The Syrian News Agency accused Aoun of being behind the Mufti's assassination.

During the same month, an Arab Summit held in Morocco suspended the Sexpartite Committee's work and established a new tripartite committee involving Saudi Arabia, Morocco, and Algeria. This committee secured Iraqi President Saddam Hussein's commitment to cease military support for Aoun and the Lebanese Forces. Additionally, the Palestinians supported Syria's adversaries.

As Syrian and allied Lebanese forces bombarded residential areas, seaways, and fuel warehouses in an attempt to exert control over East Beirut, the Lebanese Army units under Aoun's command and the Lebanese Forces fought back. Innocent civilians bore the brunt of the conflict. In late July 1989, the Tripartite Arab Committee accused Syria of obstructing its work.

In response, Washington closed its embassy in East Beirut, severing ties with Aoun's government. Despite these challenges, efforts to reach an agreement to end Lebanon's war continued, with Maronite Patriarch Nasrallah Sfeir and the Lebanese Forces leader, Samir Geagea, participating in negotiations.

On September 30, 1989, Lebanese parliamentarians convened in the Saudi city of Taif to negotiate an agreement to end the war. Aoun agreed to allow parliament members living in his controlled areas to leave. After three weeks, 62 Lebanese parliament members gathered in Taif and endorsed the National Reconciliation document.

Subsequently, in the town of Klayaat, Rene Mouawad was elected President on November 22, 1989. However, Aoun's supporters blamed Samir Geagea and Maronite Patriarch Sfeir for their setback, leading to a forcible entry into the Maronite Patriarchate and compelled the patriarch to kiss Aoun's picture. Sfeir subsequently moved to his summer residence in an area under Syrian control.

President Mouawad extended an olive branch to Aoun, proclaiming in his inaugural speech that reconciliation was inclusive. Tragically, on Independence Day, November 22, 1989, an explosion killed President Mouawad while passing through West Beirut. Once again, Syria accused Aoun of being responsible. Two days later, Lebanese Parliament elected Elias El-Hrawi as Mouawad's successor. El-Hrawi called on Aoun to step aside, prompting thousands of Lebanese to stage a sit-in at Aoun's residence, which they named the "Palace of the People."

Arab representative El-Akhdar El-Ibrahimi strived to broker an agreement to halt the destructive shelling but felt that Aoun's enemies were working to negate his efforts.

By late January 1990, violent clashes erupted between the Lebanese Army, under Aoun's command, and the Lebanese Forces militia, leading to what was termed the "War of Elimination." The two sides engaged in a deadly struggle, resulting in numerous civilian casualties.

This conflict weakened General Aoun and drew Geagea closer to the camp supporting Syria. Geagea relinquished control of areas to President El-Hrawi and voiced support for the Taif Agreement, expressing optimism about the country's future.

The invasion of Kuwait by Iraqi forces on August 8, 1990, shifted regional dynamics. Iraq's focus on the aftermath of its invasion prompted Aoun to lose his last Arab ally. This development also led President El-Hrawi to enact political reforms, including granting Muslims a number of parliamentary seats equal to Christians. Efforts to end the crisis continued, with the government negotiating a document with Aoun, in which he recognized El-Hrawi's government.

The situation came to a head on October 13, 1990, when international permission was granted for Syrian aircraft to bombard Aoun's stronghold, the Ba'abda presidential palace. Syrian troops, along with Lebanese forces supporting El-Hrawi's government, stormed the East Area.

The Syrian military occupied the presidential palace and the Defense Ministry, confiscating hundreds of secret Lebanese files. Officers loyal to Aoun were arrested and transported to Syrian prisons. Seeking refuge in the French embassy and then later in French exile, Aoun's downfall seemed inevitable. Shortly after Aoun's departure, Dany Chamoun, son of the late president Kamil Chamoun, was assassinated, along with his wife and children in their home in East Beirut.

Years later, Samir Geagea was convicted of the assassinations of Chamoun, his family, Prime Minister

Rachid Karameh, and the bombing of a church. He was sentenced to life imprisonment, remaining isolated until the early 21st century.

The Lebanese army dismantled barricades and reopened roads, marking the end of the conflict. Over 15 years, Lebanese territory saw the presence of Syrian, Israeli, Palestinian, Iranian, American, British, French, and Italian forces, along with international and Arab peacekeeping forces.

The Lebanon War tore apart communities, resulting in senseless killings along religious lines. Various denominations committed atrocities against each other, and people of the same group turned against each other. Countless lives were lost in militia, regional, and international battles. Innocent blood, both Muslim and Christian, was unjustly spilled, with no gain and in vain. The war left the country in ruins, claiming the lives of 150,000 individuals.

The Aftermath: 1990-2000 Southern Conflict

After the majority of the conflicts of the Lebanese civil war came to an end following the Ta'if Accord, Israel continued to maintain a military presence in South Lebanon. This led Hezbollah to carry on with operations in the South, as they were now the dominant force in the Islamic Resistance.

In a series of Israeli air raids that concluded on June 4, 1991, several buildings owned by various Palestinian factions were targeted, resulting in the deaths of 22 individuals and the injury of 82 others. A month later, on July 4, 1991, the Lebanese Army launched an offensive in Southern Lebanon after disarmament negotiations failed, as mandated by the Taif agreement. The operation, involving 10,000 troops against around 5,000 militia, lasted three days and ended with the Army seizing all Palestinian positions around Sidon.

A total of 73 people were killed, and 200 were wounded, predominantly Palestinians.

Hezbollah's leader, Abbas al-Musawi, declared their refusal to surrender their weapons, asserting, "Our guns are a red line that cannot be crossed." This was followed by an ambush of an Israeli patrol by Hezbollah on July 16, resulting in the death of three Israeli soldiers and one Hezbollah fighter. The next day, the South Lebanon Army retaliated by destroying 14 houses and burning crops in Majd al-Zun.

Prior to their dissolution, members of the Amal militia were also active in South Lebanon. On July 29, 1991, they killed three members of the South Lebanon Army (SLA), prompting Israeli shelling that claimed the lives of two villagers. On August 23, 1991, two SLA members were killed by Amal militia, leading to Israeli retaliatory shelling that resulted in the death of a civilian and the injury of two Irish soldiers serving with UNIFIL.

More violence ensued later in 1991, with an Irish UNIFIL soldier being killed by the SLA on November 15, and three Lebanese Army soldiers dying due to an Israeli rocket on November 25.

On February 16, 1992, al-Musawi, along with his family and four others, was assassinated when Israeli AH-64 Apache helicopter gunships fired three missiles at his motorcade. This attack was in retaliation for the killing of three Israeli soldiers two days earlier. In the aftermath, Hezbollah launched rocket fire onto the Israeli security zone, prompting Israel to respond with airstrikes and sending armored columns past the security zone to strike Hezbollah strongholds in Kafra and Yater. Musawi was succeeded by Hassan Nasrallah, who declared a policy of "retribution," stating that if Israel targeted Lebanese civilian areas, Hezbollah would retaliate with attacks on Israeli territory. Meanwhile, Hezbollah continued its attacks against IDF targets within occupied Lebanese territory.

In response to these developments, Ehud Sadan, the chief of security at the Israeli Embassy in Turkey, was assassinated by a car bomb. The Islamic Jihad organization is reported to have claimed responsibility for the 1992 attack on the Israeli embassy in Buenos Aires, which resulted in 29 deaths, as a retaliatory measure.

In 1993, hostilities resumed with a month of Hezbollah shelling on Israeli towns and attacks on its soldiers, leading to a seven-day Israeli operation in July known as Operation Accountability, aimed at striking Hezbollah. The operation resulted in the deaths of one Israeli soldier, between 8 and 50 Hezbollah fighters, along with 2 Israeli and 118 Lebanese civilians. Subsequently, a mutual agreement mediated by the United States prohibited attacks on civilian targets by both parties.

Following the conclusion of Operation Accountability, a brief period of calm was disrupted by renewed light shelling. On August 17, a major artillery exchange occurred, and two days later, nine Israeli soldiers were killed in separate Hezbollah attacks. In response, Israel launched airstrikes against Hezbollah positions, resulting in the death of at least two Hezbollah fighters.

Ongoing Conflict in the Late 1990s

In the mid-1990s, tensions between Israeli forces and Hezbollah militants led to a series of retaliatory strikes and escalating violence. These events included the abduction of an Amal leader by Israeli commandos, deadly airstrikes and rocket attacks, resulting in casualties on both sides. The situation further intensified with the tragic deaths of civilians and soldiers, as well as clashes and confrontations in the region.

During Operation Grapes of Wrath in 1996, a significant number of Lebanese civilians lost their lives, particularly during the shelling of a United Nations base, despite efforts to secure a ceasefire. The conflict persisted, claiming the lives of Hezbollah fighters, Syrian soldiers, and Israeli troops.

Amid this turmoil, incidents such as an ambush on an IDF convoy and clashes between Israeli forces and Hezbollah militants continued to occur, resulting in casualties on both sides. Tragically, a significant number of Israeli soldiers lost their lives in an aviation disaster, further adding to the toll of the conflict.

Throughout 1997, Israeli special forces actively disrupted Hezbollah's activities in the security zone, engaging in successful operations to thwart infiltration attempts and eliminate key Hezbollah commanders. However, the intense clashes between IDF troops and militant groups led to further loss of life, including an unfortunate friendly fire incident that resulted in casualties among Israeli soldiers.

The ongoing violence and confrontations in the late 1990s underscored the deeply entrenched conflict between Israeli forces and Hezbollah, leading to a devastating toll on both sides.

Failed Israeli Raid in Southern Lebanon, 1997

On September 5, 1997, a mission carried out by 16 Shayetet 13 naval commandos of the Israeli Defense Forces took a tragic turn when they inadvertently walked into an ambush set by Hezbollah and Amal militants near the coastal town of Ansariye. The commandos encountered improvised explosive devices (IEDs) and came under intense enemy fire, resulting in the death of their commanding officer, Lt. Col. Yossi Korakin, as well as several other soldiers due to exploding bombs.

Following the distress call from the surviving commandos, Israel swiftly launched a rescue operation involving Unit 669 and Sayeret Matkal, utilizing two CH-53 helicopters. The rescue effort faced fierce resistance as Lebanese Army anti-aircraft units and Hezbollah militants engaged the Israeli forces. With the situation escalating, Israel intervened with airstrikes and threatened significant retaliation, compelling Hezbollah and Amal to halt their attacks.

The confrontation resulted in the loss of twelve Israeli soldiers, six Hezbollah and Amal fighters, and two Lebanese soldiers, along with an innocent civilian. In the aftermath, Hezbollah leader Hassan Nasrallah claimed that the group had intercepted Israeli reconnaissance drones to plan their ambush. Subsequent IDF raids in Lebanon led to further casualties on both sides, intensifying the already volatile situation in the region.

Escalation and Retaliatory Strikes

The violence continued to escalate, with Hezbollah employing new tactics including Sager missiles, resulting in the deaths of additional IDF soldiers and the modification of Israeli tank armor. Amidst these hostilities, Israel actively sought to disrupt Hezbollah's operations, culminating in the targeted assassination of a key Hezbollah explosives expert in 1998.

The confrontations persisted, with IDF units facing ambushes and roadside bombings, claiming the lives of senior Israeli officers and soldiers. Additionally, Hezbollah forces launched coordinated attacks on multiple Israeli and SLA outposts in south Lebanon, further contributing to the spiraling conflict between the two adversaries.

The period of 1997 to 1999 witnessed a significant surge in hostilities between Israel and Hezbollah, marking a turbulent chapter in their enduring conflict in southern Lebanon.

In June 1999, after five days of Lebanese villages in the South being targeted by artillery fire, Hezbollah launched a barrage of Katusha rockets into northern Israel, resulting in injuries to four people. The Israeli reaction was swift. On 24–25 June, the IAF carried out two prolonged waves of airstrikes. Following the initial air raids, Hezbollah responded with another rocket attack into the heart of Kiryat Shimona, claiming the lives of two individuals. The Israeli bombing caused an estimated $52 million in damages, including the destruction of five bridges on the road leading south from Beirut. The city of Beirut was plunged into darkness when the power plant at Jamhour was struck, resulting in the tragic deaths of three firefighters. This plant had been previously repaired after being hit during the Grapes of Wrath conflict. Additionally, the headquarters of a telephone company in Jieh and Hezbollah's al Manar radio station in Baalbek were also obliterated. In total, eight Lebanese lost their lives, with seventy sustaining serious injuries, including two individuals who slipped into a coma.

Moving to August 1999, Hezbollah commander Ali Hassan Deeb, renowned as Abu Hassan and a prominent figure in Hezbollah's special force, was assassinated in an Israeli military operation. Deeb was driving in Sidon when two roadside bombs were detonated by a remote signal from an overhead UAV.

Overall, during 1999, several dozen Hezbollah and Amal fighters were killed, as well as twelve Israeli soldiers and one civilian, with one casualty due to an accident.

The Withdrawal: 2000

In July 1999, Ehud Barak assumed office as Israel's Prime Minister, vowing that Israel would unilaterally withdraw to the international border by July 2000. This commitment defied prior expectations, as many believed that Israel would only pull out from South Lebanon upon reaching a consensus with Syria.

In January 2000, Hezbollah carried out the assassination of Colonel Aql Hashem, the commander of the South Lebanon Army's Western Brigade, at his residence in the security zone. Hashem, who had overseen the day-to-day operations of the SLA and was a top contender to succeed General Antoine Lahad, was targeted in the attack. The methodical pursuit and killing of Hashim was meticulously documented and broadcast on Hezbollah's TV channel, al-Manar, dealing a severe blow to the morale within the SLA.

Throughout the spring of 2000, Hezbollah intensified its operations significantly, persistently harassing Israeli military outposts in occupied Lebanese territory. In preparation for a major withdrawal, Israeli forces began vacating several forward positions within the security zone of South Lebanon. On May 24, Israel publicized its decision to withdraw all troops from South Lebanon. By the following day, all Israeli forces had exited Lebanon, more than six weeks ahead of the previously stated deadline of July 7.

The Israeli withdrawal led to the disintegration of the SLA and the swift advancement of Hezbollah forces into the area. As the Israeli Defense Forces (IDF) withdrew, thousands of Shi'a Lebanese swiftly returned to the South to reclaim their properties. This retreat was widely perceived as a triumph for Hezbollah and bolstered its popularity in Lebanon. The completeness of the withdrawal remains contested, with the Lebanese Government and Hezbollah asserting that Israel still maintains control over the Shebaa farms, a small piece of territory on the Lebanon-Israel-Syria border, with sovereignty in dispute.

Due to the refusal of a Syrian-backed Lebanese government to demarcate its border with Israel, Israel collaborated with UN cartographers under the leadership of regional coordinator Terje Rød-Larsen to verify that Israel had withdrawn from all occupied Lebanese territory. On June 16, 2000, the UN Security Council affirmed that Israel had indeed pulled out its forces from all of Lebanon in accordance with United Nations Security Council Resolution 425 (1978).

Israel viewed this action as a tactical withdrawal, as it had always perceived the Security Zone as a buffer zone to safeguard its citizens. By terminating the occupation, Barak's cabinet anticipated an enhancement of Israel's international image. Ehud Barak contended that "Hezbollah would have gained international legitimacy in their struggle against a foreign occupier" had the Israelis not withdrawn unilaterally without a peace agreement.

The 2006 33 Day War

Between July 12 and August 14, 2006, Israel engaged in a conflict with Hezbollah forces in southern Lebanon and Beirut, utilizing land, air, and sea operations. This 34-day confrontation saw Israel conducting numerous air strikes, while Hezbollah launched missiles into northern Israel. According to Human Rights Watch, the intense conflict resulted in at least 1,109 Lebanese fatalities, with the majority being civilians, along with 4,399 injuries and approximately one million displaced individuals. HRW also reported that 43 Israeli civilians and 12 IDF soldiers lost their lives during the war.

The conflict was triggered by the 2006 Hezbollah cross-border raid. On July 12, 2006, Hezbollah fighters initiated the hostilities by launching rockets at Israeli border towns, creating a diversion for an anti-tank missile attack on two armored Humvees patrolling the Israeli side of the border fence. This deadly ambush resulted in the deaths of three soldiers, with two more soldiers abducted and taken to Lebanon by Hezbollah. In a subsequent failed rescue attempt, five additional soldiers lost their lives in Lebanon. Hezbollah's subsequent demand for the release of Lebanese prisoners held by Israel in exchange for the abducted soldiers was refused, leading to Israeli airstrikes and artillery fire on targets in Lebanon, including Beirut's Rafic Hariri International Airport. The IDF also launched a ground invasion of Southern Lebanon and imposed an air-and-naval blockade. In response, Hezbollah intensified its attacks by launching rockets into northern Israel and engaging the IDF in guerrilla warfare from fortified positions.

Hezbollah's Demands and Israeli Response

Hezbollah insisted on the liberation of Lebanese detainees in Israeli custody in exchange for the release of the two captured soldiers. However, Israel rejected the demand and instead initiated extensive ground and air offensives in Lebanon. Furthermore, Israel enforced an air and naval blockade on the entire country.

Israeli airstrikes targeted not only Hezbollah military sites but also vital civilian infrastructure, such as the Beirut airport, television and radio stations, as well as schools. According to HRW, around 7,000 bombs and missiles were launched by Israeli warplanes in Lebanon.

In response, Hezbollah retaliated by launching missiles at Israel, predominantly utilizing Katyusha missiles, initially employed by the Soviet Union in World War II. The conflict escalated when rockets struck the Haifa train depot, resulting in the deaths of eight Israel Railways employees. Additionally, other northern Israeli cities, including Safed, Nazareth, and Afula, were targeted.

The situation intensified when, on 30 July, the Israeli Air Force bombarded the village of Qana in southern Lebanon, resulting in the deaths of 28 civilians, including 16 children, with 13 individuals reported as missing. This incident echoed a previous tragic event in April 1996 when Israel targeted a UN compound in Qana, causing the deaths of at least 106 people and injuring numerous others. Following the 2006 attack, the international community heavily criticized Israel for its targeting of civilians, leading to an international outcry. Human Rights Watch also accused Israel of committing war crimes in a report released on 2 August.

Subsequent Events

On 11 August 2006, the UN Security Council unanimously approved Resolution 1701, aiming to halt the hostilities. Hezbollah's Secretary-General, Hassan Nasrallah, pledged to adhere to the ceasefire, while Israel's cabinet voted in favor of the resolution. The ceasefire took effect on 14 August, and Israel eventually lifted the naval blockade on Lebanon on 8 September 2006.

Initially, both Israel and Hezbollah claimed victory in the conflict. Nasrallah declared that Hezbollah had achieved a "divine, historic, and strategic victory," while international observers highlighted the group's survival in the face of overwhelming power as a significant public relations triumph. The war had severe economic implications, with the Lebanese government estimating direct war damages at $2.8 billion and forecasting a five percent shrinkage in the national economy, largely attributed to halted tourism.

The conflict's aftermath also had political repercussions, as it contributed to the downfall of Israel's prime minister at the time, Ehud Olmert. The war has been deemed a military failure for Israel due to its inability to disarm or eradicate Hezbollah. The Winograd Commission, appointed by the Israeli government, classified the war as a "missed opportunity" and uncovered deficiencies in the country's decision-making processes. This ultimately impacted Israeli politics, reviving Benjamin Netanyahu's career and indirectly leading to his return to power two years later.

Made in United States
Orlando, FL
16 September 2024